# MEET THE NEW CHARACTER!

The team at **BookLife Publishing** would like to congratulate **Archer Peak** and **Penelope Stevens** from **Wisbech Grammar School**, who won our design a character competition with this fantastic new addition to the world of **Charlie's Park**. We have had great fun bringing **Ronald the Poacher** to life.

# Chapter 1
## Monkeying Around

It was quiet in the rainforest clearing, and empty.

Well, not quite empty.

Halfway up a tree sat a small, scruffy, yellow-haired boy. His name was Archie. He was wearing a yellow visor over his eyes, and bright yellow gloves. It bleeped occasionally. There was a faint scent of bananas. All around

Archie, the trees were still.

Very still.

In fact… perhaps a little too still…

Archie touched his visor.

"Ook," he whispered.

The stillness shattered as thirty monkeys leapt from the trees, soaring in all directions. Some twirled! Some whirled! Some loop-de-looped!

What an amazing monkey gymnastics display! There were monkeys here! There were monkeys there! There were monkeys everywhere! Each monkey was wearing the same visor, which was faintly bleeping. One was doing the splits. It was magnificent.

Archie watched the monkeys carefully, counting

under his breath: 5... 6... 7... 8... On his visor screen, he could see each monkey in the team. As he waved his hands in a series of complicated movements, the visor followed his yellow gloves, sending signals to the team. All over the clearing, little monkey noses twitched. From their visors, tiny puffs of Banana

Number Three, the world's most irresistible banana scent, fired left and right. The monkeys, led by the smell, twirled and whirled in response. Archie could control the whole team. They had been practising for weeks. It was going brilliantly...

...until it wasn't. Archie frantically tapped the side of

his visor. The smell of burning Banana Number Three filled the air. The monkeys, some in mid-twirl, suddenly started screeching and throwing off their visors. Some wobbled. Some toppled. Some tried to hang on... But things were not going to plan.

12

"Stop! I mean – OOK!" shouted Archie. "Uncle Monty! Help!"

But it was too late. The monkeys fell.

Uncle Monty skidded into the clearing to find a heap of tangled monkeys on the ground.

"Oh dear," said Uncle Monty. "That didn't go to plan."

"Something happened to my visor again," said Archie. "Can you fix it?"

Of course, Uncle Monty could definitely fix it. He was not only Archie's uncle, but

also the park's teacher, and
resident inventor. He took
the PriM8-1000 visor from
Archie. A black puff of Banana
Number Three wheezed from
the side.

"I can fix it" Said Uncle
Monty. "But I need a 217
Gadgetron ratchet. I've got
one in the mobile lab. Wait
here." He left, muttering to

himself about banana serum injectors.

Archie turned to the monkeys. They were picking themselves up from the heap. One, a baby named Pickle, ran up his leg and settled on his shoulder. Pickle began to check Archie's hair for fleas. She was sad not to find any, so Archie gave her a banana chip from his pocket. The little monkey gobbled it up happily, smacking her lips. She patted Archie on the shoulder.

"Oh Pickle," said Archie, walking over to the heap of struggling monkeys. "If we don't get this right, we'll never win the – OOOOOKKKKK!!"

Archie was cut short as he, Pickle and the other monkeys

were suddenly swept into the air!

What was happening?

# Chapter 2
## Pigs Might Fly

Charlie pointed his phone toward the sky.

"Look, Mum! They've almost got it!" He cried.

On-screen, he could see his mum smiling as the Pink Arrows, his flying pig stunt display team, soared overhead. Sixteen pigs, each attached to a jetpack, swooped and soared in perfect formation. Coloured smoke in long lines trailed behind each pig. Slowly, as they swooped, they wrote across the sky:

CHARLIE'S PRAK

"Almost!" said Mum. "How do you train them?"

"They will do anything for a Piggy Treat," said Charlie. "It's Uncle Monty's secret recipe. They smell like Archie's socks, but the pigs will follow anywhere I throw them. I think I'm in with a chance of winning the talent show this year, you know."

"I'm very impressed," said Mum through the phone. "You'll have to work hard to beat my African elephant ballet swimming team, though. We've won the last three years, remember."

"How's Dad's act going?" The Talent-Tastic Teams Tournament was Dad's least favourite event in the park calendar. People came to Charlie's Park from miles around to see the teams compete in the tournament and vote for the winner. The best teamwork wins. Every year, Dad chose a different animal for his team, and every year he had trouble. Like the year the flamingos got their legs tangled in the middle of

the tap dancing and it had
taken three days to un-knot all
the knees.

"He was doing well," Mum said. "But he can't get the hyenas to stop giggling long enough to sing the harmonies. How is your brother doing?"

This was the first year that Charlie's little brother Archie was old enough to be in

the Talent-Tastic Teams
Tournament. Most people in
the tournament chose animals
that were smart, sensible and
could follow instructions. Not
Archie. Archie had chosen the
monkeys. Monkeys were not
known for being sensible, or
for following instructions.
Monkeys were known for
causing total chaos. But

the monkeys were Archie's favourites. Archie said just because they weren't sensible, it didn't mean they weren't smart. He hadn't let anyone see what he'd been practising, except for Uncle Monty.

Just then, Uncle Monty pulled up in the mobile lab. Charlie said goodbye to his mother and ran over. The lab shuddered to a stop and Uncle Monty clambered out. Charlie sniffed. Was that... burnt banana?

"Hello, Charlie!" boomed Uncle Monty. "I left my 217 Gadgetron ratchet in my other lab coat. Silly me!" He strode into the classroom with Charlie right behind him.

Just another day in the nature reserve the boys called home. Wasn't it?

# Chapter 3

## The Monkey Business

Back in the clearing, Archie and the monkeys had found that they were caught up in a huge net. Archie knew someone must have set a trap for them. But who would break into the park to capture a load of monkeys? Pickle squeaked and pointed to the sky. Above their heads, a hot air balloon was slowly sinking into view. The tangled monkeys started wriggling harder. Archie figured he'd better get control of the monkeys and get them all out before the balloon got much closer. He went to touch his visor – but it was missing! Of course. Uncle Monty had taken it.

"Uncle Monty!" He shouted. There was no answer. How would he get them out now?

Archie looked up as the balloon hovered low above them. Hanging out of the basket was a very, very tall man. He was wearing a tall top hat. Dangling from his long arms was a big, shiny hook on a rope. The tall man swung the hook back and forth, as if he was fishing for something.

"Ook," muttered Archie. "He's fishing for us!"

Sure enough, the man hooked the net and, with a heave, leaned back into the balloon. There was a whoosh and a roar and the balloon rose into the sky, carrying a net full of stolen monkeys (and one small boy).

Pickle tapped Archie on the shoulder. Then she pointed up. Archie nodded.

"I agree. Come on."

Archie and Pickle squeezed through the ropes, climbing over the tangled monkeys and up the rope until they reached the basket. They

peered over the top.

Sitting in the basket was the tall man, his nose deep in a book. The rest of the basket was full of tattered books. Someone had scribbled all over them in red pencil. On top of the books sat the top hat. Archie was surprised to see the man's hair stuck straight up like a pole. That explained the

tall hat, at least. This strange man even had tall hair!

The man was talking to himself. He sounded cross.

"Oh, I hate monkeys!" he said. "I have captured just about every monkey I can find. I've forced them all to work in my book factory. I've given each one a typewriter, and I've paid them peanuts." He sighed and threw the book overboard. "And they STILL haven't written a good book!"

The man picked up another book and licked the end of his red pencil. "No-one told me that getting into the Monkey Business would be so stressful. They type and type all day, and still just produce this rubbish! Hopefully these new monkeys will be a bit more... creative."

The tall man reached out a long leg and kicked an old, dusty-looking machine on the side of the balloon's basket. "SAT NAV!" he shouted. "TAKE US TO THE BOOK FACTORY."

The machine spluttered and creaked, and a large dial on the top swung around and pointed due north. The balloon headed towards the horizon. Archie and Pickle climbed back into the net and Pickle told the monkeys what they had seen.

Archie needed a plan.

# Chapter 4

Archie in the Sky with Monkeys

Back at the classroom, Charlie was starting to get worried. The last flight of the day had landed, and it was snack time, but Archie wasn't back yet. Archie never missed his afternoon banana cake.

"Perhaps we should check on him," said Uncle Monty, pulling up the classroom screen. The screen showed all

the different parts of the park.
Uncle Monty zoomed in on the
rainforest, and then down to
the clearing – just in time to
see Ronald the Poacher take
off in his balloon.

"He's stealing our monkeys!" cried Uncle Monty.

Charlie noticed a flash of blue climbing up the side of the net.

"Worse than that. He's stealing my little brother!" he cried.

Uncle Monty sprinted to the store cupboard and pulled out a jetpack. This one was a little smaller than the ones the pigs wore. In his other hand, he held a child-sized jetpack control.

"I was saving this for your next birthday, Charlie," Uncle Monty said. "But I think this qualifies as an emergency." Uncle Monty held the jetpack and helmet out towards Charlie. "Have you got plenty of Piggy Treats?" Charlie nodded. "Then, my boy, you know what to do." Uncle Monty hit the big red button on the desk and a siren wailed. Charlie could hear trotters clattering on the runway as the pigs scrambled into formation. He saluted Uncle Monty and was already firing up the jetpack as he ran onto the runway.

    Once in the sky, Charlie and the Pink Arrows quickly caught up to the balloon.

Charlie tossed piggy treats to his team, who swooped and soared through the clouds. Pigs really were born to fly, thought Charlie. Uncle Monty's voice crackled through the in-helmet radio.

"How are you doing, Charlie? OVER!" he bellowed. Charlie winced.

"Fine. We've almost caught

up to the balloon, over."

"Be careful, Charlie. If you hit the balloon and it bursts, they will all fall to the ground. OVER!"

Charlie looked at the very tall man, who was throwing suitcases full of paper over the edge of the basket. He seemed very upset. Pages covered with red ink fluttered across

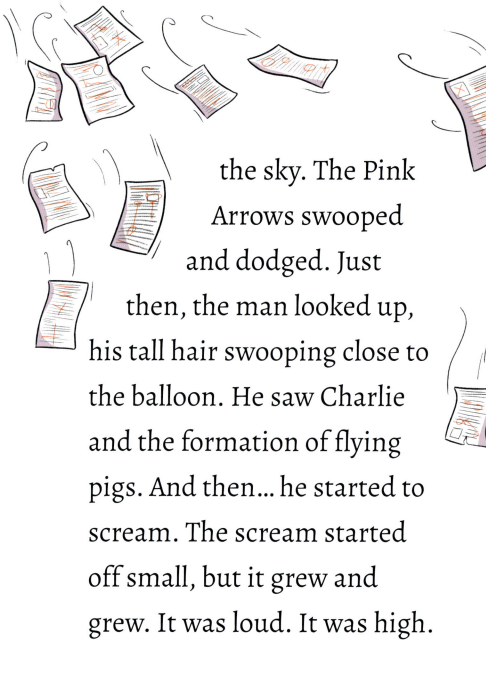

the sky. The Pink
Arrows swooped
and dodged. Just
then, the man looked up,
his tall hair swooping close to
the balloon. He saw Charlie
and the formation of flying
pigs. And then... he started to
scream. The scream started
off small, but it grew and
grew. It was loud. It was high.

It was HUGE.

ᴀᴀᴀᴀᴀᴀᴀᴀᴀᴀᴀᴀHHHHH
## NNOOOTT PIGS
# AAAARGH!!

The tall man waved his
arms and jumped up and
down. He frantically threw
everything he could at Charlie
and the Pink Arrows. A flying
suitcase narrowly missed

Marge, the lead Arrow. She narrowed her eyes at the wailing, long-armed man. Her curly tail shot out straight.

"Oh no." Charlie said. "No, Marge... Not the Rasher Crasher!"

But it was too late. Marge was hurtling directly at the man in the basket. He leapt into the air to avoid the angry

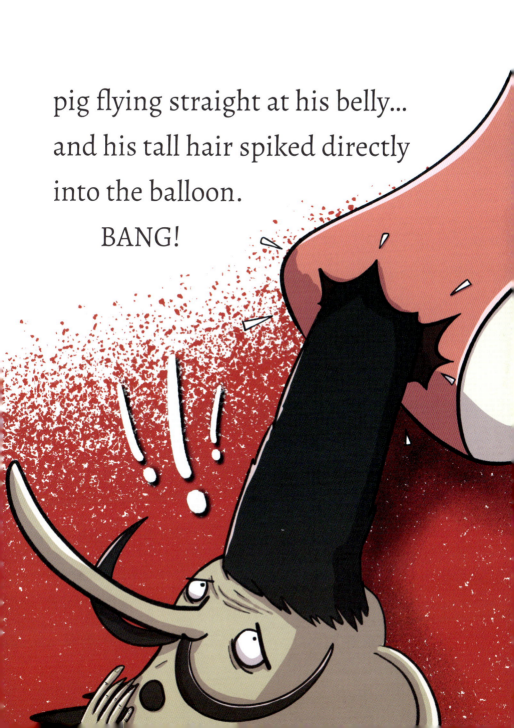

pig flying straight at his belly...
and his tall hair spiked directly
into the balloon.

BANG!

# Chapter 5

## Saved by the Bacon

Oh no! The balloon was hurtling towards the ground!

Charlie had to think fast. He emptied his pockets of Piggy Treats and threw them all after the balloon. Treats, balloon, monkeys, man and Archie all vanished into the clouds, swiftly followed by the screaming Pink Arrows hot on their tails.

Charlie held his breath.

Silence.

"Come on," said Charlie. "Where are they?"

At breakneck speed the Pink Arrows shot through the clouds, a bright rainbow of smoke trailing behind them. Each pig carried several monkeys... and one carried Archie, with Pickle clinging

onto his hair for dear life.

Marge was carrying
Ronald the Poacher, holding
his trousers very delicately
between her huge teeth.
Ronald was still screaming
and wriggling.

"Argh! Not pigs! The only
things worse than monkeys
are PIGS!" He was still
clutching a tatty book in his

hands, and he swatted at the pig with it. "Let me go let me go let me go!"

Marge rolled her eyes and let go of Ronald's trousers, just a little. Ronald slipped, screamed, and grabbed at the pig, wrapping his long arms and legs around Marge's fat belly. He closed his eyes and screamed as she winked at Charlie, saluted with a pink trotter, and sped off towards the horizon. Ronald's squealing could be heard for a long time.

Archie's pig pulled up alongside his brother. They shared a quick fist-bump. Uncle Monty's voice crackled through the radio.

"Are you boys coming

back, or can I eat all this banana cake myself: OVER!!"

# Chapter 6
## A Holiday for Ronald

The day of the Talent-Tastic Teams Tournament was bright and sunny. The jetpacks had been polished. Twenty-two enormous waterproof ballet shoes had been delivered. The hyenas were in harmony. Everyone was ready.

The monkeys were safely back at the park and recovering well from their

unexpected flight. Archie
and Charlie had rescued all
the writer monkeys from
the Monkey Business book
factory. Now, instead of
writing books, the monkeys
sold banana lollies to all the
tourists who had come to see
the show. Well, they sold most
of them, anyway...

Inside the classroom,

Archie was peeking out onto the runway. Charlie set his jetpack and helmet on the floor. He crouched next to his brother, who was nervously eating a banana chip.

"Everything OK?" he said. Archie didn't feel like talking, so he just nodded. "Are you worried?" Archie nodded again. "About Ronald?" Another nod. Charlie dragged Archie over to the screen and pushed a few buttons. "You don't need to worry about Ronald," he said. "We won't be hearing from him for a long time. He's… gone on a long holiday." Charlie giggled.

On the screen, there was a beautiful beach. The water was blue and crystal clear. The sky was scattered with wispy clouds. All over the beach were hundreds of pigs. Pigs sunbathing. Pigs swimming in the blue waters. Pigs eating piggy treats out of little cups

with umbrellas in them. Archie heard a familiar scream...
and it was getting louder. As he watched, Ronald sprinted past the camera and along the beach. He was still shrieking. Several small piglets chased playfully after him, nipping at his heels. His long legs whirled as he ran right past a pink sign stuck in the sand.